Finding Patterns

Animal Patterns

by Nathan Olson

Mankato, Minnesota

A+ Books are published by Capstone Press,
151 Good Counsel Drive, P.O. Box 669, Mankato, Minnesota 56002.
www.capstonepress.com

Printed in the United States of America

1 2 3 4 5 6 12 11 10 09 08 07

Library of Congress Cataloging-in-Publication Data
Olson, Nathan.
Animal patterns / by Nathan Olson.
p. cm.—(A+ books. Finding patterns)
Summary: "Simple text and color photographs introduce different kinds of animal patterns"—Provided by publisher.
Includes bibliographical references and index.
ISBN-13: 978-0-7368-6728-3 (hardcover)
ISBN-10: 0-7368-6728-7 (hardcover)
ISBN-13: 978-0-7368-7846-3 (softcover pbk.)
ISBN-10: 0-7368-7846-7 (softcover pbk.)
1. Pattern perception—Juvenile literature. 2. Animals—Miscellanea—Juvenile literature. I. Title. II. Series.
BF294.O5 2007
516'.15—dc22 2006018187

Credits
Jenny Marks, editor; Renée Doyle, designer; Charlene Deyle, photo researcher; Scott Thoms, photo editor

Photo Credits
Corbis/Kennan Ward, 6; Corbis/Momatiuk-Eastcott, 26–27; Corbis/Ralph A. Clevenger, 18; Corbis/Tim Davis, 21, 25; Corbis/Tom Brakefield, 10; Corbis/zefa/Frank Lukasseck, 16–17; Getty Images Inc./Stone/Art Wolfe, 4–5; James P. Rowan, 12, 22; Lynn M. Stone, 13; McDonald Wildlife Photography/Joe McDonald, 11, 20; Nature Picture Library/Brian Lightfoot, 24; Robert McCaw, 8, 9, 14; Shutterstock/Brad Thompson, 29; Shutterstock/Chris Turner, cover; Shutterstock/Lynn Amaral, 15; Shutterstock/Marc Goff, 7; Shutterstock/Matt Ragen, 23; Shutterstock/Paul Yates, 19

Note to Parents, Teachers, and Librarians

Finding Patterns uses color photographs and a nonfiction format to introduce readers to seeing patterns in the real world. *Animal Patterns* is designed to be read aloud to a pre-reader, or to be read independently by an early reader. Images and activities encourage mathematical thinking in early readers and listeners. The book encourages further learning by including the following sections: Table of Contents, Animal Pattern Facts, Glossary, Read More, Internet Sites, and Index. Early readers may need assistance using these features.

Table of Contents

What Is a Pattern?

A pattern is a repeated shape or color. Let's find patterns in the animal world.

Baby sea turtles use flippers to move, leaving behind fancy patterns in the sand.

A snail slides along as slow as can be. Its slimy trail is plainly not a pattern.

Striped and Spotted Patterns

The monarch caterpillar wears a pattern of yellow, black, and white stripes.

The monarch butterfly's
wings have a pretty pattern
of colored spots.

From whiskers to tail, black stripes wrap the tiger's body in a pattern.

The turtle's hard lower shell
has a brown-striped pattern.

Rings of dark and light fur make stripes on the raccoon's tail.

White and black stripes make
patterns on these hairy legs.
Why do you suppose this spider
is called a zebra tarantula?

A fawn's spotty pattern helps it hide in the forest. The white spots look like patches of sunlight through the trees.

A cheetah's fur has lots and lots of spots. What pattern do you see on the cheetah's tail?

Alternating Patterns

Every-other makes a pattern.
Here, every-other kitten has
soft, orange fur.

Elephants make a big and little pattern as they march along the African savanna.

Angelfish sport curvy stripes on their brightly colored scales.

Animal Action Patterns

A spider spins a pattern with silky thread. Bigger and bigger loops spread out to the web's edge.

Geese fly together in
a pattern shaped like a V.
They take turns leading
the way.

Striped bees build a pattern called a honeycomb to store their sweet, sticky honey.

Black-beaked gulls perched
above the water make a
seaside pattern.

The proud peacock's fancy tail feathers spray out in a fan pattern.

Three bottle-nosed dolphins
leap up in a side-by-side pattern.

Flocks of feeding flamingos
and pelicans make a pink-white-pink
pattern along the shore.

Animal Pattern Facts

Baby sea turtles are called hatchlings. Most of them hatch at night between July and October.

What's in snail slime? It's called mucus, which fills your nose when you have a cold. Imagine if your feet oozed slime every time you sneezed!

When fawns lie very still on the forest floor, their white spots look like patches of sunlight shining through the trees. The spotted pattern is called camouflage and it helps the fawn hide from predators.

Sumatran tigers have the most stripes and Siberian tigers have the fewest. No two tigers have the exact same pattern of stripes.

Pelicans and flamingos might eat at the same shore, but they have different ways of finding their food. A pelican dives down and scoops up fish and water in the pouch under its beak. Flamingos sip water and swish it around in their mouths to filter out algae to eat.

After spinning a web, the spider rests in the center at night and waits to catch a meal. If the spider is still hungry in the morning, it will eat the web and spin a new one in the evening.

A savanna is a tropical grassland. The weather alternates from rainy summers to dry winters. Animals like elephants, giraffes, lions, kangaroos, and zebras live on savannas. Which of these animals have patterns?

Glossary

alternating (AWL-tuhr-nate-ing)—going from one thing to another in a rhythm or pattern

caterpillar (KAT-ur-pil-ur)—a wormlike animal that changes into a butterfly or moth

flipper (FLIP-uhr)—the wide, flat limb of a sea animal

honeycomb (HUHN-ee-kohm)—a wax structure made by bees to store honey, pollen, and eggs

pattern (PAT-uhrn)—a repeated shape or color

savanna (suh-VAN-uh)—a flat, grassy area of land with few trees

tarantula (tuh-RAN-chuh-luh)—a large, hairy spider

web (WEB)—a very fine net of sticky threads made by a spider to catch flies and other insects

Read More

Ganeri, Anita. *Animal Groupings.* Nature Files. Philadelphia: Chelsea House, 2005.

Harris, Trudy. *Pattern Bugs.* Brookfield, Conn.: Millbrook Press, 2001.

Harvey, Jayne. *Busy Bugs: A Book about Patterns.* All Aboard Math Reader. New York: Grosset & Dunlap, 2003.

Internet Sites

FactHound offers a safe, fun way to find Internet sites related to this book. All of the sites on FactHound have been researched by our staff.

Here's how:

1. Go to *www.facthound.com*
2. Select your grade level.
3. Type in this book ID **0736867287** for age-appropriate sites. You may also browse subjects by clicking on the letters, or by clicking on pictures and words.
4. Click on the **Fetch It** button.

WWW.FACTHOUND.COM®

FactHound will fetch the best sites for you!

Index